Gettin **oad**

Getting Married Abroad

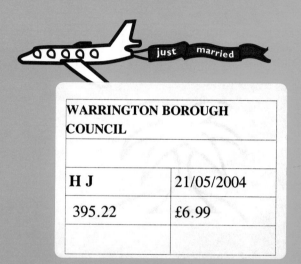

WARRINGTON BOROUGH COUNCIL	
H J	21/05/2004
395.22	£6.99

A practical guide to overseas weddings

from confetti.co.uk
don't get married without us...

First published in 2004
by Octopus Publishing Group
2–4 Heron Quays
London E14 4JP
www.conran-octopus.co.uk

Text copyright © 2004 Confetti Network Ltd;
Book design and layout copyright © 2004 Conran Octopus Ltd;
Illustrations copyright © 2004 Confetti Network Ltd

A catalogue record for this book is available from
the British Library.
ISBN 1 84091 367 3

Publishing Director Lorraine Dickey
Senior Editor Katey Day
Assistant Editor Sybella Marlow
Art Director Chi Lam
Designer Victoria Burley
Assistant Production Controller Natalie Moore

Other books in this series include *The Bride's Wedding*;
The Groom's Wedding; *Your Daughter's Wedding*; *The Father of the
Bride's Wedding*; *Men at Weddings*; *Wedding Readings & Vows*;
Wedding Dresses and *Wedding & Special Occasion Stationery*.

Contents

General information

Imagine a sandy beach, blue skies, a warm breeze, palm trees and the sound of the sea gently lapping on the shore...

If the vision that this conjures up in your mind is the epitome of romance, then getting married in an exotic location is for you. Or maybe you prefer the idea of marrying beside an Italian lake, on a US ski slope or in a safari park? Whatever you long for, it will be available somewhere in the world – and this book can help you to arrange it.

Marrying abroad can bypass all the headaches of invitation lists, venues, flowers, transport and so on. It can also be much cheaper!

Introduction

With more predictable weather, and over £10,000 cheaper than the average UK wedding, getting married abroad is a hugely appealing option to many couples. In fact, 61 per cent of couples surveyed in a Confetti poll admitted they had considered eloping during the wedding planning process!

However, many people are put off by the red tape, the complexities of organizing everything from a distance, and the fear that the marriage might turn out not to be legally valid. In fact, there has never been a better, easier or more popular time to get married abroad, so if it's always been your fantasy, don't be dissuaded from turning it into a reality.

Nowadays there are many overseas wedding packages available. If you decide to use a wedding coordinator or specialist company, this book will help you ask the right questions, make the right decisions and steer your other preparations in the right direction. It also covers matters of etiquette and common questions about gift lists, invitations and more.

If you prefer to arrange your holidays independently, it is possible to arrange your own wedding abroad with careful extra planning. This book offers practical guidance to all the documentation you'll require and all the rules and regulations you need to know about in order to organize your own successful wedding abroad, be it in the sun or the snow, up a mountain or on the beach.

Where to start

The fuss-free way to organize a wedding abroad is to book with a tour operator who specializes in arranging such events. These companies have dedicated wedding personnel who can answer all your queries and arrange every possible detail for you.

It is also quite possible to arrange your own wedding abroad. This book will help you with researching any legal requirements and residency rules, and with organizing all the finer details for yourselves, from the ceremony to the flowers. If you prefer to be in control, then your first step will be to contact the consulate or embassy of the country where you intend to marry in order to seek their advice.

These are the top ten wedding destinations researched by brides on Confetti.co.uk. Details of all these destinations and more can be found on pages 45–125.

1. Italy
2. Florida
3. Hawaii
4. Mauritius
5. Thailand
6. Las Vegas
7. St Lucia
8. Seychelles
9. Fiji
10. Mexico

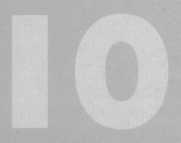

Is it right for us?

Weddings abroad are popular with couples who have been bitten by the travel bug; couples who are shy or simply don't want a fuss; couples getting married for the second time; couples who got engaged abroad, and couples with either very small or very large families. The former want to make it special with just a few guests, the latter often want to escape a huge family wedding!

You are bound to disappoint some members of your family and friends who cannot be with you on the day, especially grandparents who may feel unable to undertake such a trip. To soothe any hurt feelings, you could arrange to have a blessing service or reception on your return. At the very least, make sure you have a video made of the day so that you can share your special moments with those unable to be with you.

If getting married abroad sounds right for you, check out the main points for and against, before you make up your mind.

For

- It's much cheaper than the average British wedding, which now costs over £15,000. Many couples buy their own tickets, and the bride's dad simply pay for the wedding package – it's acceptable for guests to pay their own way.
- You can invite just a small number of people you really want to celebrate with.
- If you book through a travel operator, they'll do practically all of the organizing. If, on the other hand, you opt for a tailor-made wedding, you can become very involved in the planning process.

Against

- If it's just the two of you, strangers will have to act as witnesses. Afterwards, some couples can regret not inviting their family members.
- Some guests you want to invite may not be able to afford the ticket, and you may upset people you don't invite.
- You won't have as much control over the organizing as you would at home, and even if you head for tropical climes, you can't guarantee sunny weather.
- Unless you both head off for a second week somewhere else, you might be stuck on honeymoon with your family!
- Be aware that hotels in exotic destinations perform more than one marriage ceremony a day, and you could also be the main attraction for hotel guests. If you want to be certain of a private ceremony then consider a quieter or more unusual destination.

The legal low-down

Residency & legal requirements

Most countries have rules about residency before you can get married (check the detailed breakdown for each destination), but the usual requirement is only a few days. If you are using a tour operator, the legalities of your wedding will be dealt with by them. If you are arranging everything yourself, you will need to get accurate advice from the consulate or embassy of the country concerned.

Here's a rundown of the kind of documents you may need to supply (details of the documents required for specific destinations can be found at the end of the book). Usually you need to send copies in advance (sometimes with an *apostille* – a stamp that legalizes British documents for use abroad) and then produce the originals when you arrive.

- Birth certificates
- Valid ten-year passports
- Affidavit/statutory declarations confirming single status
- Decree absolute (if you are divorced)
- Former spouse's death certificate (if you are widowed)
- Parental consent (if you are aged under 18, or 21 in some countries)

Translation & legalization

Bear in mind that some countries, such as Greece, require translations of documents. If you use a coordinator or wedding package company this will be organized for you. Otherwise, consult the Foreign and Commonwealth Office for assistance in this matter.

Legalization/apostilles

Legalization simply means confirming that a signature, seal or stamp appearing on a document is genuine. The signatures or seals of British public officials (such as solicitors, notaries public and registrars) on certain documents from the United Kingdom have to be confirmed before those documents can be accepted overseas. To legalize a document, an apostille, or legalization certificate, is attached to it.

The Foreign and Commonwealth Office can legalize documents by post or in person. The fee for legalization in 2003 was £12 per document. If you are not sure which documents you need to legalize, you should contact your wedding planner or check the details for your chosen destination in this book.

Affidavits/Statutory Declarations

An affidavit or a statutory declaration is a legal document
that can be obtained from a Commissioner for Oaths (a
solicitor authorized to authenticate oaths on statements
etc, listed in the Yellow Pages under 'Solicitors, notary and
conveyancing'). It is important to note that single status
statutory declarations must be made individually (not
jointly). These must state that you are both free to marry
and that you are single, divorced or widowed, and must be
signed and stamped by a solicitor. They should also contain
your full name, address, nationality, religion, passport number
and occupation. This document must be obtained within
three months of your intended date of marriage and must
also state your intent to marry in the destination you have
chosen. The cost will vary from area to area, depending on
court charges, so it is well worth phoning around.

Sample:
'I (name, nationality, passport number and occupation)
do solemnly and sincerely declare as follows:
I declare that I have always been known by the name…
I also declare that I understand that I am free to contract
marriage according to the legal requirements for marriage
in (destination), and I make this Solemn Declaration
conscientiously believing the same to be true and by virtue
of the provisions of the Statutory Declaration Act 1835.
Declared by (name) at (address) and (date) signed by
(solicitor's name and official stamp).'

Certificate of No Impediment

Some countries ask for a Certificate of No Impediment, which is obtainable from the register office in the area where you reside. You will have to give notice of your marriage in the same way as you would for a civil wedding in the UK, and after 21 days you will be issued with the certificate. You will then probably be required to send a copy of the certificate to the authorities where you plan to marry, taking the original with you when you travel.

If you have changed your name

If your (legal) name is different from the one on your birth certificate for any reason other than a previous marriage, you may need to bring your deed poll certificate.

Medical tests

Some countries will require that you have a GP's certificate attesting that you are free from certain communicable diseases (usually syphilis); others, such as Mexico, will require that you take a blood test once you arrive in the country.

Divorce limitations

A few countries stipulate that a divorced person may not marry until a certain number of days have elapsed after the finalization of their divorce. Mexico (again!) generally requires a year to have passed after the issuing of a decree absolute; Mauritius has a mandatory pregnancy test for any woman who has been divorced for less than 300 days.

Is our marriage legal in the UK?

As long as your marriage is legally recognized (validly contracted) in the country where it takes place, it is deemed to be valid in England and Wales. However, in the light of the Mick Jagger and Jerry Hall marriage in Bali, which was found to be unlawful in the UK, the Law Society advises that anyone getting married abroad should contact the local British embassy or consulate for up-to-date advice. Do not rely on travel agents or any third party to ensure that the ceremony is valid; check it for yourself and be sure of what you are doing. If you are not completely satisfied that your marriage will be recognized in the UK, then visit a register office in Britain to be doubly sure. On your return home, you do not need to register your marriage with the register office. You can use your foreign marriage certificate to change your name on your documents and with your bank, as you would if you had married in the UK. It is a good idea to obtain several copies of your marriage certificate, just in case you lose the original, as it is very difficult to get further copies at a later date.

Registration in the UK

Marriages solemnized in a foreign country cannot be registered in the UK; however, it is possible, in some instances, for a record of your marriage to be kept at:

The ONS General Register Office
Overseas Section, Snedley Hydro
Trafalgar Road
Southport PR8 2HH
Tel: 0151 471 4801
Fax: 01633 652 988
Email: overseas.gro@ons.gov.uk

Passports & visas

You should ensure that you have a valid ten-year passport and, since many countries require expiry dates on passports to be a considerable length of time after the return from holiday, it is recommended that you ensure your passport is valid for six months after your return to the UK. You cannot change your name on your passport in advance if you marry abroad. Purchase your tickets in your pre-marital name.

In most cases where visas are required, the responsibility for obtaining them lies with you. The cost, method of obtaining a visa and time necessary to process applications vary considerably between countries, and are subject to change. Contact the relevant embassy at the earliest opportunity for the most up-to-date information.

Marriage certificates

Your marriage certificate may not be in English. As you may
need an English version, you should arrange for a certified
translation to be made when you return home. Usually
(depending on how much of a flying visit you make!) you
receive your marriage certificate before you return home.
In some locations, however (especially in the Caribbean), it
takes between one and six months to process the paperwork.
If this is the case, you should arrange for the final document
to be mailed to you in the UK. If you use a wedding package
company, they will arrange this for you.

Marriage blessings abroad

If you are already married, whether recently or 25 years ago,
many companies offer tropical blessings and renewal of vows
services to celebrate your union. The only legal requirement
is that you take along your original marriage certificate for
authentication, although some destinations will require you
to send a photocopy of your certificate at least six weeks
before you travel. Most of the services that are provided for
weddings can be requested for your blessing service.

Marriage blessings at home

If you are planning a blessing once you return to the UK, you
must have your marriage certificate, so check when you will
receive yours. There is no point in planning a blessing for the
week after you get back, only to find that your certificate is
still in the post!

Proxy weddings

It is possible to get married abroad without actually leaving your house. In a marriage by proxy, a third party stands in for one or other of the principals. The wedding of Russian cosmonaut Yuri Malenchenko and Ekaterina Dmitriev (he was on the International Space Station, she was in Houston) was the first time many people had heard of such ceremonies. They're not new, however: Napoleon married his second wife by proxy in 1810.

While proxy marriages are no longer common in Europe, the American states of Texas, Montana and Colorado all offer legally recognized ceremonies. Texas and Colorado require one party to be present and the other to verify their identity and consent by phone; Montana, meanwhile, will allow you to marry entirely without the other party.

Taking matters even further, two countries allow you to be married entirely by mail order. In Mexico and Paraguay, couples can marry in the absence of both parties, as long as the proxy has the required paperwork.

Planning your wedding abroad

When should you book? Try to book a minimum of 12 weeks before departure to allow enough time for arrangements to be made and necessary documentation completed. In some countries, such as Greece and Spain, paperwork must not be more than three months old. There will then be more administration to be completed once you arrive at your destination, which can take up to three days – but see page 45 for a list of places where you can tie the knot more quickly. If you are getting married through a tour operator, you will probably need between two and five days to complete paperwork 'in resort', so it's best to go for a fortnight. That way you can make the final arrangements while still allowing plenty of time after the ceremony to relax and enjoy your honeymoon.

How to plan

First, decide whereabouts you want to marry. Not a problem if you've always had your heart set on, for example, Zell am See or Sorrento, but if your thoughts are more along the lines of 'on a beach in paradise', now's the time to get more specific.

To do this, start by making a list of the things that are important to you at your wedding. For example:

- Not more than eight hours' flying time
- Nice weather in December
- Beach wedding
- Remote
- Religious ceremony

Once you've established this, you can find further information from the following sources:
- The Confetti travel channel – www.confetti.co.uk/travel
- Other brides – try the message boards at www.confetti.co.uk/cafe
- Travel agents
- The Internet
- Wedding magazines
- Travel supplements of national newspapers
- Recommendations of friends and family

Having found a destination that suits your requirements (and there will be one, even if you don't find it immediately!), you need to establish where you want to stay, hold the ceremony and have the reception (or wedding breakfast). If you plump for an all-inclusive wedding in the Caribbean, these may all be in the same place, or if you opt to use an overseas wedding planning company, the choice may be narrowed down for you. Again, create a list of your 'must-haves', say:

• Enough rooms in the hotel for all the wedding party
• Restaurant overlooking the sea
• Ceremony and reception venues within walking distance

If it is a practical possibility, it's often a good idea to visit your destination in advance to check out your locations and talk to local suppliers face-to-face. Obviously, if the whole idea is to have two dream weeks in the Seychelles, then you won't want to go on a fact-finding mission beforehand and spoil the whole treat. If you are relying on secondary sources for your information, you might want to hear from someone who knows the hotel, or restaurant, or florist.

The Confetti message boards are a great place to find brides who have married abroad or who are planning to marry in destinations all over the world, and who are eager to share their knowledge and experience.

What to wear?

What you wear for your wedding is naturally up to you, and there are no real dress rules if you are marrying in the grounds of your hotel. However, if you have arranged for a religious service in a chapel or church, you will almost certainly be expected to respect local customs such as covering your head and shoulders. In some eastern countries, such as Thailand, there is a specific dress code. Your tour operator or the relevant embassy will advise you.

The bride's outfit

If you have chosen to marry in tropical climes, choose a dress that will afford you maximum comfort in the heat. The traditional style of wedding outfit worn in the UK may not be practical for a beach wedding: not only will you have to contend with your dress dragging in the sand, but heeled shoes offer the potential for real disaster, as you sink backwards at an angle of 45 degrees... If you really want a full-skirt dress, wear it without the layers of petticoats for maximum cool. Otherwise, choose a short dress with shoestring straps or a lightweight, loose-fitting trouser suit. Brave Pamela Anderson types can even sport a white bikini under a sarong! For Lapland or other chillier lands, you can go wild in faux furs, bonnet and cloak. If you're slipping away to tie the knot with minimum fuss, a smart new (and re-wearable!) outfit will be more than acceptable.

Read *Wedding Dresses,* also in this series, for more ideas and inspiration.

The groom's outfit

If you're thinking of sand between the toes, there's a whole range of options available to you. In the linen suit department, there's everything from Man from Del Monte/ Pierce Brosnan chic to *Miami Vice* crushed casual style. Just remember: light shirts, no ties, panama hats optional. This may even be the opportunity to splash out on a custom-made silk suit (though it's a bit impractical).

If you want to smarten up your act a bit, a white tuxedo is great for overseas weddings in hot climates. Team a white jacket with black trousers; a white pleated-front evening shirt and black bow tie. Shoes should be black and well polished. According to the rule book, white socks should never be worn – but it's your wedding, after all. Wear white trousers, a blue silk shirt and no shoes if you want!

Or there's the Tommy Lee bathing suit or David Beckham sarong option. A word of caution: just remember your family will almost certainly want to see the photos.

Transporting & caring for your outfits

Check with your airline for advice on transporting your wedding outfits. Some recommend that they should be boxed or packed into separate suitcases, which are then stowed in the hold. Others suggest you use suit-carriers, which, space permitting, can be hung in the cabin. Outfits can always be carried as hand luggage, but this won't leave much space for anything else you may want to keep with you on the flight.

As soon as you arrive at your hotel, unpack your wedding outfits and hang them up. A warm and humid tropical climate should encourage creases to fall out naturally, but your hotel or your wedding representative can normally arrange for your outfits to be pressed, if necessary. Or try hanging them in a steam-filled bathroom, or (with care) use a hair dryer.

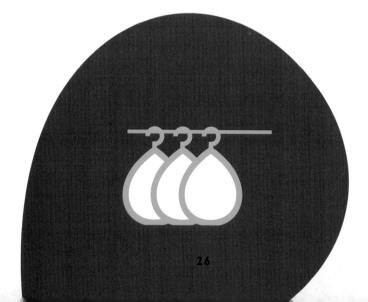

Hair & beauty treatments

Hair and beauty treatments can normally be arranged when you arrive at your hotel. If it does not offer these facilities, you can make appointments through your representative at a nearby hotel or beauty salon. For complete peace of mind, practise styling your own hair and make-up before setting off.

If you have chosen to marry in a hot climate, do beware of the sun. Wonderful though you may look wearing your wedding dress with a tan, it's all too easy to end up looking like a lobster with a mayonnaise dressing! Pace your sunbathing on the run-up to your wedding to give yourself a radiant glow, or give nature a helping hand with a good-quality fake tan.

Packing checklist

Along with the paraphernalia usually taken to your chosen destination, don't forget:

- The rings
- All your documentation
- The bride's dress, jewellery and shoes
- Skin care products and cosmetics
- The bridegroom's outfit
- Outfits for the wedding party
- Gifts for the bridesmaid and best man
- Place names, order of service, table decorations, disposable cameras
- The speeches!

A good tip is to take with you anything you may want to keep. For instance, cake toppers provided at your resort may well get recycled for the next couple, so if you want them as a memento, bring your own!

Vows

In many places – for instance in Europe – you will make your vows in the local language, so you will either have to demonstrate you can understand the native tongue well enough to follow the service or use a translator. Bear in mind that the vows won't be a direct copy of the UK equivalents.

If you are having an English language ceremony, you might be able to include your own vows, depending on whether the wedding is civil or religious. This also depends on the location – if you're marrying in a romantic garden in Los Angeles for instance, you're probably going to have more time to do the personal stuff than if you're queuing up at the Little White Chapel in Las Vegas.

Check in advance – if you are not using a coordinator, then your celebrant will be able to help you out. If you decide to write your own vows, then you may wish to consult *Wedding Readings & Vows* in this series, which will give you more help and suggestions.

29

Inviting guests

Broadly speaking, weddings abroad fall into three categories: those where the bride and groom tie the knot with Elvis or a New York taxi driver as witnesses; those where the bride and groom are accompanied by one or two friends or close family, and those where the bride and groom do their utmost to get everyone they know over to Skiathos or Ravello for the kind of wedding similar to they'd have at home, only with more sun.

Wedding guest lists are potentially a tricky subject, and nowhere more so than when an invitation implies a financial commitment on the part of the guest. Very few couples can afford to pay for transport and accommodation for all the guests, and few guests will expect this. When inviting guests to a wedding abroad it always makes sense to have organized a few travel arrangements before hand, whether this is simply giving them the name and number of the travel consultant who is organizing your wedding, or supplying them with a list of flights and hotels.

Obviously if you ask people to book flights and hotels abroad and you cancel or postpone the wedding, you may cause them a fair amount of incovenience and financial distress. Encourage them to buy travel insurance as soon as possible.

As with hotels at home, it is often possible to reserve a block of rooms at a preferential rate. Make sure you agree a date until which the hotel will hold the rooms, and remind your guests about this deadline!

Invitations

These can be worded in the same way as a UK wedding invitation, but you will need to send them out much earlier. Alternatively, you can send out a Save the Date card and information pack (containing details of the destination, flight, accommodation and so on) in advance, and then send the invitations out as a formality between six and twelve weeks before the date. Read *Wedding & Special Occasion Stationery,* also in this series, for more ideas.

The wedding party

The size of the wedding party is entirely up to you. Most countries require two witnesses to a marriage, but – unless you're going for an impromptu ceremony in the middle of the Amazon rainforest – this is usually easy to arrange on the spot. In fact, many wedding package companies will offer their coordinator as a witness, or even include witnesses (and in some cases bridesmaids) in the package.

You may want to involve more people, however, such as a best man or chief bridesmaid, and as weddings abroad are popular with couples getting married the second time around, children are often on the scene. Bear in mind that most ceremonies abroad will be different from the British model, so the role of the best man may not be the same, or there may not even be such a role. When you're reviewing the format of your chosen ceremony, remember to check details such as this.

If you want to include your children in some way, perhaps by asking them to give a reading, you will need to check what is expected and accepted at your ceremony. At your reception you can do whatever you like, of course, so if it's difficult or impossible to select an appropriate reading for the ceremony, your reception could be a great opportunity for your children to contribute.

Receptions at Home

Late receptions – held after the day of the wedding – are becoming increasingly popular with those getting married abroad, who want to hold a big knees-up for friends and family when they return home.

According to traditional etiquette, a reception that is held after the day of the wedding should not be referred to as a wedding reception, but rather as a party or reception held in honour of the recently married couple. At least sticking with this tradition means that people are less likely to be offended that they were invited 'only' to the reception and not the wedding, and more likely to be pleased that you are having a 'bonus' party!

Invitations to late receptions should read 'in honour of':

Mr and Mrs [bride's parents' names]
request the pleasure of your company at a dinner reception
in honour of
Mr and Mrs [bride and groom's names]
on [date]
at [time]
at [venue]

However, you can always break with tradition and base your invitations and reception on a theme around the place where you got married!

Announcing your wedding

Traditionally, wedding announcements are made by the bride's parents, but it is perfectly acceptable for wedding announcements to be sent by the bride and groom. Announcements are generally sent to family and friends who were not sent invitations. They should always be sent after the wedding has taken place, never before. Any time up to a year after is acceptable.

The bride's parents have 'the honour of announcing' or 'have the honour to announce'. It is acceptable simply to 'announce the marriage of their daughter' for less formal announcements, though this could be construed as implying the bride's parents' disapproval of their new son-in-law.

The year should be included, as the announcements are sent after the event. It should be written in words ('two thousand and four'), with the name of the church or venue underneath.

Example

Mr and Mrs [bride's parents' names]
have the honour of announcing
the marriage of their daughter
[bride's name]
to
Mr [groom's name]
on [day and date]
at [year in words]
at [venue]

Staying healthy

The last thing you want for your wedding is to be laid low by a dodgy tummy, or to spend a fortnight scratching at mosquito bites. With a few precautions and a little common sense, you can stay healthy and make this your holiday of a lifetime!

Be sensible: check you have all your immunizations well before you set off. Most injections will be available via your GP, but occasionally some that are in short supply have limited outlets, so check in advance. Have your injections at least two weeks in advance to allow them to take their full effect, and to give any allergic reactions time to settle before you set off. Some vaccinations can give you cold or flu symptoms, and the last thing you want is to feel poorly during your busiest planning times.

Avoid holiday tummy upsets by taking the usual precautions: drink bottled water (make sure the bottle has a sealed cap), peel fruit yourself and always eat thoroughly cooked foods. Avoid ice and salads.

Sunstroke is pretty unpleasant, and to be avoided at all costs. Loose, comfortable clothing is always the best cover-up in strong sunlight. Always use a protective sunscreen. When choosing sunglasses look for the British Standards label BS2724: 1987, wear a wide-brimmed hat and avoid sunbathing in the middle of the day. Avoid sunbathing altogether before your wedding day – you don't want to go red, or get unexpected and unattractive stripes or start to peel!

If you're doing the deed on a skiing holiday, or you're at an all-inclusive resort surrounded by tempting water sports, don't indulge until after the event. You don't want to be sporting a broken arm in your pictures – or worse, not be there at all because you're in the local hospital.

Finally, don't forget to take out insurance (a surprisingly high number of honeymooners lose their wedding rings to the sea!). You may want to upgrade from your normal insurance to cover the dress, jewellery and other expensive items.

Gift lists

The most frequently asked question about gift lists in conjunction with weddings abroad is: 'should we have one?' Obviously, if you are having a very limited guest list and no plans for a party on your return, then it would be inappropriate to send a gift list round with the announcement of your wedding! But what is the etiquette if you are having a late reception on your return?

In general, your friends and family will certainly want to buy you a present to help you start married life together, and it's always easier for both the giver and recipient if there is a wedding list. However, it might not be taken well if you send a gift list out with a wedding announcement and party invitation. Although it is becoming quite acceptable to enclose a gift list with a wedding invitation, for the sake of convenience, it should not be enclosed with an invitation to a party or late reception. After all, you didn't invite these people to your wedding – would you expect them to invite you to a party and send a gift list? But by all means keep a supply of gift cards to send to those who ask.

Wedding packages & tour operators

Tour operators can often organize everything as part of a wedding package. Some companies offer to sort the wedding arrangements for free (especially if it's part of a group booking), but typically, ceremony prices start from around £50, rising to £500 with flourishes such as a steel band or traditional dancers. Extras featured in premium wedding packages may include a morning bike ride with the hotel manager (Barbados); a 'Just Married' door message (Cuba); or two Balinese bridesmaids (Bali). Obviously it's up to you which of these you can't live without!

The service is nearly always a civil one, although religious ceremonies and blessings can be arranged in most destinations. Most hotels have an area specially set aside for conducting wedding ceremonies, and there are some more adventurous possibilities, including exchanging vows underwater or on skis in the Alps.

What's included?

Packages tend to include only your basic requirements, but these differ from company to company and hotel to hotel. Generally, you may expect them to include the following:

- Wedding ceremony
- Marriage licence and certificate
- Registry fees
- Bride's bouquet
- Groom's buttonhole
- Wedding cake
- Sparkling wine
- An appropriate location
- Coordination and organization of all of the above

If you want extras such as photography or a video, then expect to pay more. Remember that any such extras will generally be of a fairly basic nature compared to what you might expect if marrying at home. Always check in the brochure or with your tour operator for details.

The wedding cake

If the wedding cake is being provided, check what kind it will be. It's often just a sponge cake with simple pink or white icing, but this will depend on local availability. For instance, in Cyprus you will usually get a decorated fruit cake, but in Greece, a sponge cake. There are UK companies who make cakes especially for overseas weddings and will pack them appropriately for travelling.

Look in the Confetti Supplier Directory for details at www.confetti.co.uk/confetti_pages/default.asp

Flowers

Your tour operator may ask you to choose your wedding flowers before you go. As many flowers are seasonal it will be necessary to discuss your requirements at an early stage. If possible wait until you arrive at your destination to decide what you want so that you can have a clear idea of what is available. Alternatively, you may like to consider taking a bouquet and headdress of silk or dried flowers that have been made up in the UK

Witnesses

If witnesses are required, the company representatives at your destination are usually more than happy to oblige.

41

Questions to ask the planner

- What exactly is included in the wedding package?
- Where will the ceremony take place, and does the hotel restrict the number of weddings that take place each day? Is the legal side properly covered? (Check the destination details which start on page 50.)
- What time of day is it possible to get married?
- Will you be offered a discount if you bring family and friends with you?
- Will you be in contact with a planner in the UK or abroad? If abroad, get an email address for easy communication across different time zones.
- Will the ceremony be conducted in English or will you need a translator?
- Can the airline guarantee your party will be seated together on the plane?
- Will you be able to carry your dress onto the plane as hand luggage?

- Can the hotel arrange a cake?
- Can the hotel arrange a photographer and video?
- Will the wedding venue be decorated?
- Can music be provided?
- Is any food included?
- What happens if it rains? Can the date of your wedding be changed, or is there an indoor venue?
- Will you receive your marriage certificate during your honeymoon, or will it be sent to you?
- Will you be the only couple getting married at the hotel that day?
- Can you take out extra wedding insurance on top of your standard honeymoon insurance?
- Does the hotel have a hair and beauty service?
- Can an extra room be provided for you both to get ready in separately?

Inspiring ideas

Ten places to tie the knot on the spot

Requiring passports only and no residency
- Florida
- Los Angeles
- Las Vegas
- Antigua

Requiring passports only and one to three days' residency
- Alaska
- Bahamas
- New York

Requiring passport and birth certificate, a short residency or none at all
- Hawaii
- Thailand
- Cayman Islands

Ten 'aisles' in the sun

- **Santorini (Greece)** – the Med provides 'something blue' for this island wedding destination

- **Jersey (Channel Islands)** – where better to celebrate than on this island of the rich!

- **St Lucia (Caribbean)** – rainforest, a volcano, coral islands and romantic sunsets...

- **Magnetic Island (Australia)** – a tropical setting in the Great Barrier Reef World Heritage Marine Area

- **Monkey Island (UK)** – a private island in the middle of the Thames' reached by footbridge or boat

- **Key West (Florida)** – also hosts same-gender commitment ceremonies

- **Mauritius (Indian Ocean)** – the classic palm-fringed island location and Mark Twain's 'blueprint for heaven'

- **Burgh Island (UK)** – make your vows in an Art Deco hotel on an island 200 metres off the south Devon coast

- **Isle of Wight (UK)** – an absolutely fabulous location (Joanna Lumley's son was married here)

- **Bali (Indonesia)** – a favourite of countless couples

Ten ways to do it differently

- Enjoy a fairytale wedding at Disney World. Arrive in Cinderella's glass coach and have your photos taken with Mickey and Minnie Mouse!

- Opt for a drive-in wedding in Las Vegas – pull up at the hatch, and a minister will marry you through the window!

- In a hot-air balloon drifting over the South African plains

- Once you've tied the knot, bungee jump-start your marriage with a leap off Skipper's Bridge in New Zealand

- Head east for a traditional Buddhist ceremony in Thailand

- Enjoy a snowy ceremony atop America's Heavenly Mountain, then ski down the slopes as husband and wife

- The Swiss lakes were made for romance – get married by tying the knot overlooking Lake Geneva.

- In the legendary Amsterdam Hilton room where John and Yoko staged their love-in for peace in 1969

- On the concourse of Sydney Opera House, overlooking the majestic harbour

- Marry on an idyllic South Pacific island – you can't go far wrong with Bora Bora or Fiji

Destinations

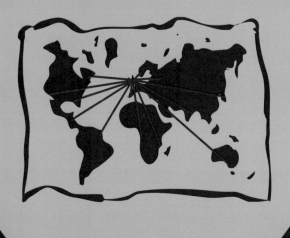

On the following pages are details of how to get married in some of the world's most popular destinations. We list information on how to obtain a marriage licence and other legal documents required by these countries. It may save you from discovering too late that you can't fulfil the requirements for a specific country. Not all places will be able to offer the wedding ceremony you expect. This is especially true of religious weddings. Some countries, such as France, recognize only civil weddings, and some wedding companies organize only civil ceremonies around the world.

A word of warning: don't try and cheat protocol or due process when planning your wedding abroad. Remember, a marriage is a legal ceremony, and you don't want to find yourself doing a Mick Jagger and Jerry Hall. If the country of your dreams is not listed here, contact the relevant Embassy or Consulate in question for details.

Europe

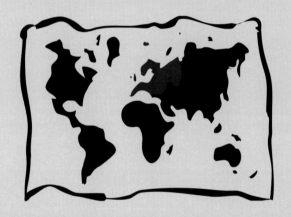

Europe – yes, that includes the UK – has some of the most inconvenient residency rules in the world. For instance, one country demands seven days' residency before you even apply for a marriage licence, which then takes 15 days to process, meaning you have to wait a whole 22 days before you get married – and, yes, that's England. France and Spain are two of the most popular destinations for weddings in Europe, and it's not difficult to see why – most of us have probably spent at least one idyllic holiday in one or other of them. However, they have very similar residency requirements to the UK, and this means that, for most couples who do not live in those countries, it's not as easy as they might have hoped. But there are plenty of other gorgeous places where you can tie the knot, and here are just a few – plus details on France and Spain for you gluttons for punishment!

Austria

Residency
There is no minimum residency requirement.

Legal requirements
Proof of ID: Your original birth certificates and passports will be required.

Proof of status: A Certificate of No Impediment must be obtained from your local register office not more than six months before your wedding date.

Divorced: If either of you is divorced, you must produce your decree absolute.

Widowed: If either of you has been widowed, you must produce the death certificate of your deceased spouse.

Age restrictions: The minimum age to marry without parental consent is 19 years old. If you are younger, then you must obtain evidence of parental consent in the form of a sworn affidavit.

Name change: If you have changed your name by deed poll, you must provide legal proof, stamped and signed by a solicitor. This also applies if you are a divorced woman and have reverted to your maiden name.

Ceremonies

Austrian law recognizes only civil marriages, but a religious ceremony may be performed after a civil marriage has been solemnized. Civil marriages are performed by officials of the Vital Statistics Office in the appropriate jurisdiction, and may be followed by a religious ceremony, if you desire. It is sometimes possible to arrange to have your civil ceremony somewhere other than in a register office, such as on a mountain side, but this is down to the individual registrar. If you have a particular preference, ask in advance.

Obtaining a marriage licence

You should apply for your marriage licence at the Standesamt of the first district of Vienna. You must both attend in person, taking all necessary documents with you. Originals or certified copies of documents must be sent to the register office where the marriage is to take place, at least eight to ten weeks before your intended date of marriage. Any affidavits and your Certificate of No Impediment must be translated into German first.

Useful contacts
Austrian Embassy
18 Belgrave Mews West
London SWIX 8HU
Tel: 020 7235 3731
Fax: 020 7344 0292
Email: embassy@austria.org.uk

Flight time: 2 hours
GMT: +1 hour
Visa: not required

Cyprus

Residency
Three days in order to sort out paperwork once you arrive.

Legal requirements
Proof of ID: Full birth certificates.

Divorced: A certified copy of the decree absolute is required. This certificate must have a coloured court stamp.

Widowed: A death certificate must be presented.

Name change: If you have changed your name by deed poll, you must produce the original stamped document.

Adoption: If you are adopted, you must produce your adoption certificate.

Age restriction: If either of you is under 18, written consent from your parent or guardian will be required.

Ceremonies
Anglican weddings: Cyprus has a number of Anglican churches. Before the wedding, you should meet with the vicar and assure him or her that you are intending to marry for the right reasons. In certain locations, one of you will have to present a baptism or christening certificate, so check before you go.

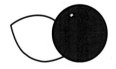

Catholic weddings: You need to advise your parish priest in the UK of your intent to marry abroad, and put him in touch with your celebrant in Cyprus in order to organize your documentation. Cypriot Catholic weddings must be preceded by a register office wedding.

Civil weddings: These are held in the register office of the town where you are staying.

Obtaining a marriage licence

When you arrive in Cyprus, you will need to take original copies of all your documents to the register office to register your intent to marry. A Declaration of Oath (proof that you're free and single to marry) will be prepared here, and this needs to be legalized in the court house. You then return to the register office to read the oaths to a witness and reconfirm the day, date and time of the wedding. The same procedure is followed for both religious and civil ceremonies.

Useful contacts

Cypriot Embassy
93 Park Street
London W1Y 4ET
All enquiries tel: 020 7499 8272
Tourist information tel: 020 7569 8800

Flight time: 4½ hours
GMT: +2 hours
Visa: not required

France

Residency
One or both of you must reside in the *département* (district) or the *arrondissement* (if in Paris) for at least 30 days before the marriage. Following these 30 days, French law requires the publication of the marriage banns at the *Mairie* (town hall) for 10 days. Thus 40 days is the minimum period of residence before a civil ceremony can take place.

Legal requirements
Proof of ID: Certified birth certificates issued less than six months before the date of the marriage and your passports. A pre-marital certificate, which is obtained at the *mairie* (town hall) where the wedding will take place.

Proof of status: A pre-marital certificate, obtained at the *mairie* (town hall) where the wedding will take place. Prenuptial certificates of good health issued by a medical doctor less than two months before the date of the marriage, to cover: serological tests for syphilis, irregular antibodies, rubella and toxoplasma.

Personal certificates of celibacy (provided by your embassy). Notarized Affidavits of Law, drawn up by a solicitor in the state of residence of the parties, stating that: the person is free to marry, and the marriage performed in France will be recognized as valid in the home country.

A certificate of residence (provided by your embassy).

All documents must be translated into French. The translations and the original documents must be verified by the French

Consulat Général. Foreign documents must be legalized before being presented to the French authorities. Obtaining an apostille will legalize documents.

Divorced/widowed: If you have been married before, a certified copy of the death certificate of the deceased spouse or a certified copy of the decree absolute is required.

Ceremonies

In France only civil weddings are legally recognized. Religious ceremonies have no legal standing. If you want to marry in a French church, then you will also have to go through a civil ceremony at another venue. Alternatively, you could consider having a civil marriage at home and then a religious wedding in France.

Obtaining a marriage licence

On arrival in France you should contact the *mairie* to start the process.

Useful contacts
Maison de la France
178 Piccadilly
London W1V 0AL
Tel: 0906 824 4123 (60p/min)
Fax: 020 7493 6594
Email: info.uk@franceguide.com
Website: www.ambafrance.org.uk

Flight time: 1 hour
GMT: +1 hour
Visa: not required

Greece

Residency

The rules differ slightly depending on which island and in which town you are getting married. Please contact the register office in the town in which you wish to wed for full details. It will take around three days to complete all your paperwork once you have arrived in Greece.

Legal requirements

Proof of ID: Full birth certificates are required.

Proof of status: A Certificate of No Impediment should be obtained from your local register office. It may take up to one month to obtain but must not be issued more than three months before your wedding day.

Divorced: If either of the parties is divorced, the decree absolute must be presented. The certificate must have a coloured court stamp.

Widowed: If either of the parties is a widower, a death certificate must be presented.

Name change: A full deed poll certificate must be presented.

Adopted: If either of the parties is adopted, an adoption certificate must be presented.

Apostille: This certifies the legalization of all your documents (see page 13 for how to obtain it).

All documents must be officially translated into Greek and then forwarded to the Greek Consulate.

Ceremonies

Civil ceremonies: The documentation listed opposite should be sent to the register office in which you intend to marry between one to two months before your wedding.

Catholic weddings: You need to advise your parish priest in the UK of your intent to marry abroad and put them in touch with your celebrant in Greece in order to organize your documentation.

Orthodox: One of the parties must be Greek Orthodox and both must have been baptized. Documentation varies between parishes, so always check.

Obtaining a marriage licence

On arrival, you should visit the local municipality in Greece where the ceremony is to take place, to fill out the application form and collect the marriage licence. Two announcements must also be made in a daily Greek newspaper (one for each party).

Useful contacts
Consulate General of Greece
1A Holland Park
London W11 3TP
Tel: 020 7221 6467
Fax: 020 7243 3202
Website: www.greekembassy.org.uk

Flight time: 3 hours
GMT: +2 hours
Visa: not required

Italy

Residency
Some municipalities require you to sign a Declaration of Intent to Marry, two to five days beforehand, so always check.

Legal requirements
Proof of ID: Your full birth certificates and ten-year passports will be required for proof of identity.

Proof of status: A Certificate of No Impediment must be obtained from your local register office.

Divorced: An official copy of your decree absolute will be required. A divorced woman may not remarry within 300 days of the dissolution of her previous marriage.

Widowed: If either of you has been widowed, you will need to produce the death certificate of your deceased spouse.

Age restriction: You must both be 18 or over to marry in Italy. If you are below this age, you must obtain parental consent in the form of a sworn affidavit.

Civil ceremonies: Civil weddings in Italy may only be performed in a register office, but most town halls are housed in historic buildings that offer a lovely setting for a wedding. The ceremony lasts about 30 minutes and is conducted in Italian. An interpreter will be needed throughout both the ceremony and for the Declaration of Intent to Marry. Contact the Italian Consulate for details of register offices and how to arrange for an interpreter.

Religious ceremonies: A Roman Catholic ceremony can be performed in most cities and will be registered automatically with the Italian authorities. Some areas will perform marriages of mixed religion, as long as you have obtained a dispensation from your parish priest. Ceremonies for other religions can also be arranged, but are not recognized by the Italian authorities and require a prior civil ceremony. This can take place either in Italy or at home before you travel.

Obtaining a marriage licence

A Certificate of No Impediment must be obtained from your local register office and sent, along with photocopies of the first five pages of your passports and your original birth certificates, to the British Consulate in the Italian city where you wish to marry. You will then be issued with a *Nulla Osta*, which you take to the register office on your arrival. Allow at least three months for the paperwork to be completed, as Italian bureaucracy is notoriously slow and complicated.

Useful contacts
Italian Consulate
38 Eaton Place
London SW1X 8AN
Tel: 020 7235 9371
Fax: 020 7823 1609
Email: itconlond@btconnect.com
Website: www.embitaly.org.uk

Flight time: 2–3 hours
GMT: +1 hour
Visa: not required

Lapland

Residency

Lapland is not an actual country, but a region covering the northern parts of Finland, Sweden and Norway. One full working day is the residency requirement. These regulations apply to Finnish Lapland.

Legal requirements

Proof of ID: Full birth certificates.

Proof of status: A Certificate of No Impediment should be obtained from your local register office. It may take up to one month to obtain but must not be issued more than three months before your wedding day.

Divorced: If either of the parties is divorced, the decree absolute must be produced. The certificate must have a coloured court stamp.

Widowed: If either of the parties is widowed, a death certificate must be produced.

Name change: A full deed poll certificate must be produced.

Adopted: If either of the parties is adopted, an adoption certificate must be presented.

Apostille: This certifies the legalization of all your documents (see page 13 for how to obtain it).

Age restriction: Both parties must be over 18 years old.

Ceremonies

The registrars of the local register offices carry out civil marriage ceremonies. The marriage ceremony can be short and no-frills, but can also include live music and poetry readings. At least two witnesses must be present at any marriage ceremony. A church blessing can be carried out in addition to the civil ceremony, if agreed with the church parish. An investigation is carried out prior to a marriage in order to ensure that there is no reason why the marriage may not be carried out. The investigation can be carried out by either the local register office or an appropriate church parish. The Certificate of No Impediment must be left at the local register office before the marriage. In addition, the bride and groom must inform the local register office of the surname or surnames they plan to use.

Obtaining a marriage licence

You should contact the register office in the area in which you wish to marry for further details.

Useful contacts

Finnish Embassy
38 Chesham Place
London SW1X 8HX
Tel: 020 7838 6200
Fax: 020 7235 0680
Website: www.finemb.org.uk/en/

Flight time: 3 hours
GMT: +2 hours
Visa: not required

Malta

Residency
Two full working days is the residency requirement.

Legal requirements
Proof of ID: Full birth certificates are required.

Proof of status: Affidavits to affirm single status.

Divorced: If either of the parties is divorced, the decree absolute must be presented. The certificate must have a coloured court stamp. You will also need an affidavit to declare your marital status, stamped by a notary.

Widowed: If either of the parties is widowed, a death certificate as well as your previous marriage certificate must be presented.

Name change: A full deed poll certificate must be presented.

Adopted: If either of the parties is adopted, an adoption certificate must be presented.

Apostille: This certifies the legalization of all your documents (see page 13 for how to obtain it).

Ceremonies

Civil weddings can be celebrated in the Marriage Registry itself, which is situated at 26 Old Treasury Street, Valletta. A civil marriage may also take place at any other place open to the public and which the registrar accepts as appropriate.

Religious weddings are celebrated in the church of the appropriate denomination. You should make certain of the place of marriage before requesting publication of banns. Bear in mind that in order to make any changes in the notified place of marriage, the Marriage Registry requires at least three weeks' notice.

Obtaining a marriage licence

Once you have confirmed your wedding, you need to obtain forms RZ1 and RZ2 from the Marriage Registry and complete and return them no less than six weeks before the wedding date. Once in Malta, you must visit the register office two to three days before the wedding to present passports and details of witnesses (who must be over 18).

Useful contacts

The Marriage Registry (Malta)
26 Old Treasury Street
Valletta
CMR 02
Malta
Tel: 00 356 21 221 775
Fax: 00 356 21 249 234

Flight time: 5 hours
GMT: +3 hours
Visa: not required

Spain

Residency
To marry in Spain, you generally need to be resident in the consular district where the wedding is to take place 21 days beforehand. However, this varies, so do check in advance.

Legal requirements
Proof of ID: Full birth certificates are required.

Proof of status: A Certificate of No Impediment should be obtained from your local register office. It may take up to one month to obtain but must not be issued more than three months before your wedding day

Divorced: If either of the parties is divorced, the decree absolute must be presented with a coloured court stamp.

Widowed: If either of the parties is widowed, a death certificate must be presented.

Name change: A full deed poll certificate must be presented.

Adopted: If either of the parties is adopted, an adoption certificate must be presented.

Application form: This must be signed by both parties and indicate the full name, occupation, domicile or residence, and citizenship of the contracting parties and their parents. This form is available from the Civil Registry or the District Court of the bride's residence.

Apostille: This certifies the legalization of all your documents (see page 13 for how to obtain it). All documents must be translated into Spanish and authenticated by the Spanish Foreign Ministry.

Religious ceremonies: Spanish law now recognizes Catholic, Protestant, Islamic and Jewish marriages as valid without the need for a second civil marriage. Regulations may vary depending on the religious denomination. Religious marriages are a matter for the relevant church authorities in the area of the forthcoming marriage, and should therefore be consulted about their requirements well before the date of the intended marriage. To be accepted as valid under Spanish (and UK) law, such a marriage must subsequently be registered with the local civil authorities. It is therefore important to confirm that the particular church involved (or priest) is licensed to marry and to establish the arrangements for civil registration.

Further information
Application for a civil marriage should be made to the:

British Consulate General
Paseo de Recoletos 7–9   **Flight time:** 2–3 hours
4th Floor   **GMT:** +1 hour
20884 Madrid   **Visa:** not required
Tel: 0034 397 3700
Fax: 0034 913085201

Outside Madrid, apply to the District Court of the bride's or groom's residence, which ordinarily assumes jurisdiction.

Switzerland

Residency
No residency or waiting period is required to get married.

Legal requirements
Proof of ID: Your full birth certificates and ten-year passports will be required for proof of identity.

Proof of status: A statutory declaration and a Promise of Marriage form (obtainable from the Swiss Embassy) must be completed and presented to the Swiss Embassy in London a minimum of four months before the intended date of marriage.

Divorced: An official copy of your decree absolute will be required. A divorced woman may not remarry within 300 days of the dissolution of her previous marriage, unless she has meanwhile given birth to a child.

Widowed: If either of you has been widowed, you will be required to produce the death certificate of your former spouse.

Age restriction: You must both be 18 or over to marry in Switzerland. If you are below this age, you must obtain parental consent in the form of a sworn affidavit.

Ceremonies

The Swiss recognize only civil marriages in a register office, but it is possible to have a religious marriage blessing afterwards. A romantic way to personalize your wedding is by arriving in a horse-drawn carriage, and a yodel choir could make the perfect musical accompaniment.

Obtaining a marriage licence

Before a marriage ceremony can be performed in Switzerland, the Promise of Marriage must be published at the civil registrar's office where you plan to marry. The Promise of Marriage must be made by both of you personally on a special form (available from the Swiss Embassy in London), before either the registrar in Switzerland or a notary public or solicitor in the United Kingdom. If the Promise of Marriage and/or the statutory declaration is made in the UK, the notary's or solicitor's signature must be legalized by the Foreign and Commonwealth Office in London.

Useful contacts
Swiss Embassy
16–18 Montagu Place
London W1H 2BQ
Tel: 020 7723 9581
Fax: 020 7724 7001
Email: swissembassy@lonirep.admin.ch
Website: www.swissembassy.org.uk

Flight time: 1½ hours
GMT: +1 hour
Visa: not required

North America

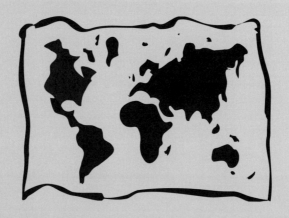

Be aware that each state has different laws. You should check out thoroughly the marriage laws of the state you set your heart on. Also, few states will accept an 'out of state' marriage licence, so you can't get a licence in Denver, for instance, and motor up to Boston for the ceremony.

Some states – including Mexico – will require a blood test. In the past, this was used to check the couple weren't closely related, but now it is usually to check for HIV status or syphilis. If you test positive, you won't get a marriage licence. Many of the more popular wedding destinations, however, lifted the blood-test requirement some time ago.

Alaska

Residency
There are no residency requirements, and you can avoid the three working day waiting period before a marriage licence is granted by applying by post in advance.

Legal requirements
Proof of ID: You will be required to appear in person at one of the marriage bureaux with your passports.

Divorced: A certified copy of your decree absolute will be required if your previous marriage ended within 60 days of your application.

Widowed: If either of you has been widowed, you will be required to produce the death certificate of your former spouse.

Age restriction: You must both be 18 years old or over. If either of you is below 18 you should contact a bureau office for additional instructions.

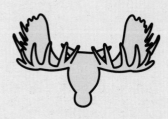

Ceremonies

You can have your wedding ceremony anywhere on land, so you can choose anything from a glacier field (via helicopter) to a chapel on a lake or at one of the many spectacular glacier gardens. If you want a religious service, you should contact the church of your choice direct. Details of churches are obtainable from Alaska Tourism.

Obtaining a marriage licence

There is a three-day waiting period before a licence can be granted. Application can be made in person, by phone, fax or letter. The waiting period begins once the necessary information is received. If your application is made by phone or fax, a hard copy of the information must follow by mail. You must provide the following: both of your names, addresses and telephone numbers, plus all the appropriate documents listed opposite. Once your licence has been issued, it is valid for 90 days. You can also fill in the application form on line at www.dced.state.ak.us and fax it to the relevant marriage bureau.

Useful contacts
American Embassy
24 Grosvenor Square
London W1A 1AE
Tel: 020 7499 9000
Website: www.usembassy.org.uk

Flight time: 10 hours
GMT: -8 hours
Visa: not required

Florida

Residency
There are no residency requirements in Florida, but you must obtain your marriage licence first (see opposite).

Legal requirements
Proof of ID: You will be required to present your passport or birth certificate.

Proof of your age: Your passports or birth certificates will be acceptable.

Divorced: If you are divorced, you must have a copy of your decree absolute, clearly indicating the date and place that the decree is registered.

Widowed: If either of you have been widowed, you must produce the death certificate of your former spouse.

Age restriction: You must be a minimum of 18 years old to marry in Florida without parental consent.

Name change: If you have changed your name by deed poll, legal proof, stamped and signed by a solicitor, is required. This also applies if a married woman has reverted to her maiden name.

Adopted: If you are adopted, the adoption certificate must be produced.

Ceremonies

If a fairytale wedding appeals to you, your dreams can come true in Disney World – but, in true American fashion, Florida offers you so much more as well. Here you can have whatever type of ceremony you desire, from 30 feet underwater at a Key Largo reef to a quiet romantic setting in a lakeside gazebo, or a religious service in one of Florida's beautiful chapels. Legally recognized marriage ceremonies can be performed by all regularly ordained ministers of a church, and all judicial officers, clerks of the circuit courts and notaries of the state.

Obtaining a marriage licence

All you have to do to obtain your marriage licence is attend the clerk's office in person, taking with you all necessary documents and the fee, which is currently $88.50. Once the application is filed, the licence is issued immediately. The process normally takes no more than 15 minutes and the licence is then valid for 60 days from the date of issue.

Useful contacts
American Embassy
24 Grosvenor Square
London W1A 1AE
Tel: 020 7499 9000
Website: www.usembassy.org.uk

Flight time: 9½ hours
GMT: -5 hours
Visa: US visa or waiver form required

Hawaii

Residency

There are no residency or citizenship requirements, but two full working days may be required to process documents in some instances.

Legal requirements

Proof of ID: You both need a valid ten-year passport and copies of your birth certificates.

Divorced: You must produce your decree absolute if you are divorced.

Widowed: If either of you has been widowed, the death certificate of your former spouse will be required.

Name change: If you have changed your name by deed poll, the original, stamped document must be produced.

Age restriction: The legal age for marriage is 18 years, but with the written consent of both parents, legal guardian or family court, it is possible to marry as young as 15.

Ceremonies

Ceremonies can be held indoors, in a church, chapel or hotel, or under the sky in a beautiful location. You could take a helicopter flight into the forest, or even write your vows in the sunken remains of a ship! In Hawaii, just about anything goes.

Obtaining a marriage licence

Application to marry must be filed with a marriage licence agent in the state. Both of you must appear personally before the marriage licence agent, as applications cannot be made by post. The licence is valid for 30 days from the date of issue.

Useful contacts
The Hawaii Visitors' Bureau
PO Box 208
Sunbury-on-Thames
Middlesex TW16 5RJ
Tel: 020 89414009
Email: vmoore@hvcb.org
Website: www.gohawaii.com

Flight time: 16½ hours
GMT: -10 hours
Visa: yes

Las Vegas

Residency
There are no residency requirements for marrying in Las Vegas, but a marriage licence is required.

Legal requirements
Proof of ID: You must present some identification and proof of your age – your passports or birth certificates will be acceptable.

Divorced: If you are divorced, you must have a copy of your decree absolute, clearly indicating the date and place that the decree is registered.

Age restriction: You must be over 18 years old, although you can marry at 16 or 17 if you are accompanied by at least one of your parents or if you have an affidavit confirming your parents' permission. Proof of age will be required up to the age of 21.

Ceremonies
There are as many types of wedding ceremony in Las Vegas as there are places to get married. You can have anything from a short simple civil ceremony to an elaborate, romantic wedding. The simplest way to get married is at a brief civil ceremony performed by the Las Vegas Marriage Commissioner, which takes only half an hour and will cost about $50.

Wedding chapels are part of the myth of Las Vegas, and most casinos contain chapels that are very elegant and far grander than the smaller independent chapels, which means there is something to suit all tastes. For an unforgettable wedding, you could try one of the wedding services offered by local wedding consultants. You can choose anything from an Elvis or Star Trek theme to a ceremony held flying in a helicopter perched on the rim of the Grand Canyon!

Obtaining a marriage licence

You must both appear in person at the Marriage License Bureau at 200 South Third Street, downtown. The office is open from 8am until midnight on weekdays and from 8am Friday until midnight Sunday every weekend. It is also open 24 hours on all holidays. Once you have your licence, any person authorized in the state of Nevada can perform the marriage ceremony, which must take place within one year of the date your licence is issued.

When you return home, you will require a copy of your Nevada marriage certificate as proof of your marriage: this can be purchased at the Clark County Recorder's office.

Useful contacts
American Embassy
24 Grosvenor Square
London WIA IAE
Tel: 020 7499 9000
Website: www.usembassy.org.uk

Flight time: 10 hours
GMT: -8 hours
Visa: US visa or waiver form required

Los Angeles

Residency
You do not need to provide proof of residency to marry in Los Angeles. A marriage licence can be obtained on the same day, provided it is collected by 3pm.

Legal requirements
Proof of ID: You must provide proof of identity in the form of your passport or driver's licence.

Divorced: If you are divorced, you must have a copy of your decree absolute, clearly indicating the date and place that the decree is registered.

Widowed: If either of you has been widowed, you must produce the death certificate of your former spouse.

Age restriction: You must be a minimum of 18 years old to marry in Los Angeles without parental consent.

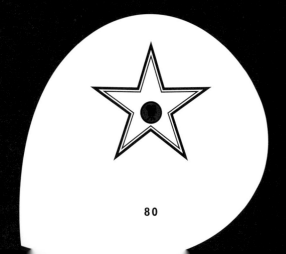

Ceremonies

You may wish to exchange your vows in one of the magical
worlds of Disney Land, but Los Angeles has so many other
possibilities to offer as well. Whether you choose to marry
in a chapel or a beautiful garden, or to star in your own
Hollywood blockbuster, it's all there for the asking. Ordained
ministers of a church, judicial officers, clerks of the circuit
courts and notaries of the state can perform legally
recognized marriage ceremonies.

Obtaining a marriage licence

Your licence can be picked up from a number of offices
in the city. It may be obtained up to 90 days before your
wedding date, and you must both be present with the
necessary documents when you make the application.

Useful contacts
American Embassy
24 Grosvenor Square
London W1A 1AE
Tel: 020 7499 9000
Website: www.usembassy.org.uk

Flight time: 11 hours
GMT: -8 hours
Visa: US visa or waiver
form required

Mexico

Residency
No Mexican residential requirements apply, but you should allow a few days for legal checks.

Legal requirements
Blood tests and x-rays: You must have a blood test done in Mexico; the Civil Registers Office can recommend a doctor or clinic.

Proof of ID: Your original birth certificates*, valid ten-year passports and entry permits are all required.

Proof of status: You must both attend your local register office in the UK (seven days' residency in the district is required) and give 'notice of marriage'. After 21 days, a Certificate of No Impediment* will be issued (£25). This certificate is valid for three months.

Divorced: A divorced person cannot marry in Mexico until one year after the divorce has been finalized (this may vary in different areas and proof of divorce may be enough). You must provide your decree absolute* with a court stamp.

Widowed: If either of you has been widowed, you must produce the death certificate* of your former spouse.

Age restriction: You must both be over18, otherwise you will need permission from a parent or legal guardian.

Name change: If you have changed your name by deed poll*, you must provide legal proof, stamped and signed by a solicitor. This also applies if a married woman has reverted to her maiden name.

All documents marked * must be translated into Spanish by
a legal translator and certified by the Legalization Department
at the Foreign and Commonwealth Office in London.

Ceremonies
In Mexico, only civil marriages are recognized as legal.
You may have a religious ceremony but it will have no
legal validity. A civil wedding is fully valid for legal purposes
worldwide, but a religious wedding without a civil
ceremony is not.

Obtaining a marriage licence
Marriages are performed at the Oficina del Registro Civil
(Civil Registers Office) for a fee, which can range from $100
to $250 in resort areas. Every city and town has an office.
Most people in these offices do not speak English, which is
where a wedding coordinator comes in handy if you don't
speak Spanish. The ceremony can be performed elsewhere,
but you will need to check with the office for information
and extra fees.

Useful contacts
Mexican Consulate
8 Halkin Street
London SW1X 7DW
Tel: 020 7201 0970
Website: www.mexicanconsulate.org.uk

Flight time: 11½ hours
GMT: - 6 hours
Visa: not required

New York

Residency
One day.

Legal requirements
Proof of ID: Full birth certificates.

Divorced: A certified copy of the decree absolute is required.

Widowed: A death certificate/previous marriage certificate must be presented.

Name change: If you have changed your name by deed poll, the original stamped document must be produced.

Adopted: If either of you is adopted, the adoption certificate must be produced.

Age restriction: If either of you is under 16, written consent from your parent or guardian will be required.

Ceremonies

There is no particular form or ceremony required except that the parties must state in the presence of an authorized member of the clergy or public official and at least one other witness that they take each other as husband and wife. The person performing the ceremony must be registered with the City of New York in order to perform a ceremony within the New York City limits.

Obtaining a marriage licence

A couple who intend to be married in New York State must apply in person for a marriage licence to any town or city clerk in the state. The application for a licence must be signed by both the bride and groom in the presence of the town or city clerk. A representative cannot apply for the licence on behalf of the bride or groom. The marriage licence is issued immediately but the marriage ceremony may not take place within 24 hours of the exact time that the licence was issued.

Useful contacts
American Embassy
24 Grosvenor Square
London W1A 1AE
Tel: 020 7499 9000
Website: www.usembassy.org.uk

Flight time: 8 hours
GMT: -5 hours
Visa: not required

India & Africa

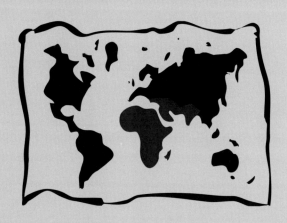

Destinations in India and Africa are increasingly popular with couples who want to combine their wedding and honeymoon with a trip of a lifetime, and for two-centre weddings. Unless you are a seasoned independent traveller, well used to planning and booking all your accommodation, flights and transfers yourself, it's probably best to go with an experienced company when booking these weddings.

Kenya

Residency
In normal circumstances residency in Kenya is 21 days. If this is not possible, a special licence can be obtained beforehand by contacting the Registrar's Office in Kenya. In this instance, no period of residency is required.

Legal requirements
Proof of ID: You will need to produce your original birth certificates and valid ten-year passports.

Proof of status: A statutory declaration must be obtained stating that you are both single and free to marry. This must be stamped and sealed and state the words 'solicitor', 'notary public' or 'Commissioner for Oaths'. Handwritten documents are not accepted.

Divorced: If you are divorced, you must produce your decree absolute with a court stamp.

Widowed: If either of you has been widowed, you must provide the death certificate of your former spouse.

Age restriction: If you are aged under 21 years, you must obtain parental consent in the form of a statutory declaration, stamped and signed by a solicitor.

Name change: If you have changed your name by deed poll, you must provide legal proof, stamped and signed by a solicitor. This also applies if you are a divorced woman and have reverted to your maiden name.

Ceremonies

You can choose between a religious ceremony in a church or a civil ceremony in a register office or, much more exciting, a safari park, but you should contact the Registrar General for a special licence specifying your desired venue. If you want a religious ceremony, you should contact your church for arrangements and information regarding the requirements.

Obtaining a marriage licence

To obtain a special marriage licence, contact the Registrar General in Nairobi with copies of the necessary documentation.

Useful contacts

Kenya Tourist Board
Notcutt House
36 Southwark Bridge Road
London SE1 9EU
Tel: 020 7202 6373
Fax: 020 7928 0722
Email: kenya@hillsbalfour.com
Website: www.magicalkenya.com

Flight time: 10 hours
GMT: +3 hours
Visa: An entry visa is required by all visitors. This can be obtained from the Kenyan High Commission in London or on arrival in Kenya.

Mauritius

Residency

For a civil wedding, you must be resident in Mauritius for 24 hours before the ceremony and must sign an affidavit at the register office to confirm that you are both free to marry. If you have chosen a religious ceremony, you must be resident for 15 days before the ceremony.

Legal requirements

Proof of ID: Your original birth certificates and valid ten-year passports are required.

Divorced: Divorcees need to produce a decree absolute. If the bride has been divorced for less than ten months, she will need to take a pregnancy test.

Widowed: If either of you has been widowed, your former spouse's death certificate and your previous marriage certificate must be produced.

Age restrictions: If either of you is under 18 years old, evidence of parental consent in the form of an affidavit, stamped by a notary, must be produced.

Name change: If you have changed your name by deed poll or have reverted to your maiden name after divorce, you must provide legal proof, stamped and signed by a solicitor.

Religious weddings: In addition to the above documents you will be required to produce your christening certificates, and a certificate of 'Good Morality' from your respective parish priests, specifying that you are both free to marry and not divorced.

Ceremonies

If you are having a civil ceremony, you must send photocopies
of your documents to The Registry, Civil Status Division
E Anquetil Building, Sir S Ramgoolam Street, Port Louis,
Mauritius, telephone 00 230 201 1727 and you must take
the originals with you for submission on your wedding day.
If you have chosen to have a religious wedding, your original
documents will be required six weeks before (or eight
weeks if you are of different religions, as the case must
go to your local bishop).

Obtaining a marriage licence

Once you arrive in Mauritius, you must go to the main
Registrar's Office to sign an affidavit to confirm that you
are both free to marry. If you have chosen to have a religious
ceremony, your original documents will be required six
weeks before you marry and eight weeks if you are of
differing religions.

Useful contacts
Mauritius Tourism
  Promotion Authority
32 Elvaston Place
London SW7 5NW
Tel: 020 7584 3666
Fax: 020 7225 1135
Email: mtpa@btinternet.com
Website: www.mauritius.net

Flight time: 12 hours
GMT: + 4 hours
Visa: not required

The Seychelles

Residency
You must normally be in the Seychelles for 11 days before your wedding, but you can obtain exemption by applying for a special licence generally issued two days after application. Your marriage can be solemnized immediately afterwards.

Legal requirements
Proof of ID: Your original birth certificates and valid ten-year passports.

Proof of status: You are required to obtain a certified affidavit declaring that there is no lawful impediment or hindrance to the marriage.

Divorced: If either of you is divorced, you will need to produce your decree absolute with a court stamp.

Widowed: If either of you has been widowed, the death certificate of your former spouse and previous marriage certificate will be required.

Age restriction: You must be 18 years or over.

Name change: If you have changed your name by deed poll, you will be required to provide legal proof, stamped and signed by a solicitor. This also applies if a married woman has reverted to her maiden name.

Ceremonies
These are generally civil ceremonies and can take place almost anywhere. The law does not recognize religious ceremonies, so you will be required to have a civil

ceremony, too. You should ask your local parish priest to contact a priest in the Seychelles directly, and all other formalities must be complied with.

Obtaining a marriage licence

You can make arrangements for obtaining a marriage licence with the Senior Officer of the Civil Status Office on the main island, but allow at least two months for processing the documentation. You must advise the date of your holiday, the name of the hotel where the ceremony is to take place and a preferred date (give alternatives). Your hotel must also confirm that your chosen date is acceptable and advise a suitable time of day. Send certified photocopies of the above documentation, taking the originals with you when you travel. The Civil Status Office will confirm the date of your wedding, fee details and whether further documents are required. If your ceremony is to take place at the Civil Status Office, the time and date can be pre-booked, but you must report there on arrival with your original documents.

Useful contacts
Seychelles Tourist Board
Notcutt House
36 Southwark Bridge Road
London SE1 9EU
Tel: 020 7202 6363

Flight time: 10 hours
GMT: +4 hours
Visa: not required

The Civil Status Office in the Seychelles
Tel: 00 248 383182

Sri Lanka

Residency

You will need to be resident in Sri Lanka for at least four days before the wedding.

Legal requirements

Proof of ID: You will need to produce your original birth certificates and valid ten-year passports.

Proof of status: If you are single, you must obtain an affidavit, signed by a solicitor, stating that neither of you has been previously married and that there is no legal objection to the marriage. You will also be asked to provide your full names and addresses and those of both sets of parents, plus your professions and those of your fathers.

Divorced: If either of you is divorced you must produce your decree absolute.

Widowed: If either of you has been widowed you must produce the death certificate of your deceased spouse.

Age restriction: The minimum age to marry without parental consent is 18. If you are younger, then you must obtain evidence of parental consent in the form of a sworn affidavit.

Name change: If you have changed your name by deed poll, you must provide legal proof, stamped and signed by a solicitor. This also applies if you are a divorced woman and have reverted to your maiden name.

Ceremonies

You may choose from a traditional religious Sri Lankan
ceremony, with live music from a calypso band, dancing and a
drummers' ashtaka and raban, leaving afterwards on the back
of an elephant or in a bullock cart. Alternatively, you may
prefer to marry at dusk on a moonlit beach or in the heat
of the day in your hotel garden.

Obtaining a marriage licence

You should take the originals of all the necessary documents
to the Civil Status Officer in the area where you wish to
marry, and you must also provide your full names and
addresses and those of your parents, and details of your
professions. If you are using a wedding organizer, they must
have photocopies of all the documents at least three weeks
prior to your date of travel.

Useful contacts

Sri Lanka (Ceylon) Tourist Board
26–27 Clareville House
Oxendon Street
London SW1Y 4EL
Tel: 020 7930 2627
Fax: 020 7930 9070
Email: srilankatourism@aol.com
Website: www.srilankatourism.org

Flight time: 11 hours
GMT: +6 hours
Visa: not required

The Far East
& the Pacific

Destinations such as Fiji, Australia and
Malaysia were once considered too far-flung
and complicated to even be contemplated as
wedding locations. Nowadays, tying the knot
in these exotic and distant lands is much easier,
and means that your honeymoon will surely be the
holiday of a lifetime. Some of the most famous
beaches in the world are to be found
in these countries, including Batu Ferringhi in
Penang and Kuta in Bali. But they also offer
wonderful opportunities for a 'two-centre'
wedding and honeymoon. How about enjoying
a relaxing week on the beach, followed by a
weekend in the ultra-modern setting of Kuala
Lumpur? Or perhaps you fancy tying the knot
in Australia's most cosmopolitan city, Sydney,
followed by a week on the Great Barrier Reef?
If so, then look no further...

Australia

Residency
There is no residency required, so if all your documents are in order, you can marry as soon as you step off the plane.

Legal requirements
Proof of ID: Valid ten-year passports and your original birth certificates.
Proof of status: A Notice of Intention to Marry must be obtained from the Australian High Commission before you travel.
Divorced: If either of you is divorced, your decree absolute with a court stamp will be required.
Widowed: If either of you has been widowed, you will be required to produce the death certificate of your former spouse and your previous marriage certificate.
Adopted: If adopted, you will need your adoption certificate.
Age restriction: You must be 18 years of age or over.
Name change: If you have changed your name by deed poll, you will need legal proof, stamped and signed by a solicitor. This also applies if a married woman has reverted to her maiden name.

Ceremonies

Marriages do not have to be conducted in a church or a register office, so the world is your oyster. You may like to have your ceremony at Sydney Opera House, on a tall ship, at a koala park, on a beach, in a garden or even in a church.

Obtaining a Notice of Intention to Marry

Weddings are conducted Monday to Friday, excluding public holidays. You will need to obtain a Notice of Intended Marriage from the Australian High Commission, Australia House, London WC2B 4LA telephone: 020 7379 4334. The document must be signed in the presence of and witnessed by:
• an Australian-registered barrister or solicitor, or
• an Australian-registered, legally qualified, medical practitioner, or an authorized celebrant (in Australia), or an Australian Diplomatic Officer, or an Australian Consular Officer.
Be sure to take your passport or some other form of identification with you and a fee of the sterling equivalent of Australian $10, which is charged for each signature witnessed. Once witnessed, the Notice form can be sent direct to the marriage celebrant or to friends or relatives in Australia if they are arranging the wedding. The marriage celebrant must receive the Notice at least one month and a day, but not more than six months, before the date of the proposed wedding.

Useful contacts

Australian Federation of Civil Celebrants
PO Box 2179
Bathurst
NSW 2795
Tel: 00 61 300 555 875
Fax: 00 02 6332 2125
Email: afcc@civilcelebrants.com.au
Website: www.civilcelebrants.com.au

Flight time: 19½ hours
GMT: +10 hours
Visa: yes

Bali

Residency
The residency requirement is technically a minimum of
10 days, but if wedding organizers submit marriage licence
applications on your behalf, this requirement is waived.

Legal requirements
Proof of ID: You will be required to produce your original
birth certificates and ten-year passports with six months
validity remaining from the date of your arrival in Bali.
Photographs: Five passport-size photographs are required,
with the groom positioned right and the bride left, of head
and shoulders only, with you both looking straight ahead.
Divorced: Your decree absolute with court stamp must be
produced. Divorced Catholics cannot marry in Bali.
Widowed: The death certificate of your former spouse
and previous marriage certificate are required. Widowed
Catholics cannot marry in Bali.
Age restriction: You must both be 18 or over to marry in
Bali. Under this age you must obtain written parental consent.
Catholic: You must obtain from your parish priest, a letter
of Freedom to Marry, a letter of Delegation addressed to the
Catholic church in Bali stating that your parish has no
objections to your marriage service being performed in Bali,
and a Pre-Nuptial Enquiry completed by you and your priest.
For mixed Catholic and non-Catholic couples wishing to
marry in the Catholic church, a letter of Dispensation for
Disparity of Religion is required. This can take up to six

weeks to obtain, so allow plenty of time in your planning.
Name change: If you have changed your name by deed
poll, proof, stamped and signed by a solicitor, is required. This
also applies to a divorced woman using her maiden name.
Adopted: Your adoption certificate must be produced.

Ceremonies

In Indonesia, it is not possible to have a civil-only wedding,
Only after the religious ceremony has taken place will the
Civil Office register and legalize the marriage. There are
some restrictions on locations for ceremonies – it is not
permitted to marry in a temple, and beach weddings are not
recommended unless they are on private beaches.

Obtaining a marriage licence

You will have to plan a stopover in Jakarta, where you must
go to the British Embassy to sign an affidavit swearing that
you are free to marry, and to apply for a Certificate of No
Impediment. Originals of the necessary documents must be
presented at the time of application.

Useful contacts

Indonesian Embassy
38 Grosvenor Square
London W1K 2HW
Tel: 020 7499 7661
Fax: 020 7491 4993
Email: kbri@indolondon.freeserve.co.uk
Website: www.indonesianembassy.org.uk

Flight time: 16½ hours
GMT: +8 hours
Visa: not required

Fiji

Residency
The minimum residency is one working day.

Legal requirements
Proof of ID: You will be required to produce your original birth certificates and valid ten-year passports.

Divorced: If either of you is divorced you will be required to produce your decree absolute with a court stamp.

Widowed: If either of you has been widowed, the death certificate of your former spouse must be produced.

Age restriction: The minimum age to marry without parental consent is 21 years of age. If you are under this age you will need to obtain an affidavit sworn by your father giving his consent.

Name change: If you have changed your name by deed poll, you must provide legal proof stamped and signed by a solicitor. This also applies if a divorced woman reverts to her maiden name.

Ceremonies

In Fiji you can choose to marry in a hotel, on a beach or in a church, and, for total privacy, you can even have an entire resort all to yourselves.

There are no non-denominational ministers in Fiji. For Catholic weddings, the requirements include a letter of Freedom to Marry, sent at least two to three months in advance to the Fijian priest, along with your baptism certificates. Your normal pre-wedding studies must be completed with a letter from your priest. Religious ceremonies are legally recognized under Fijian law.

Obtaining a marriage licence

You must both attend the register office with the original copies of all the necessary documents to apply for your marriage licence, which will be issued within one working day. The legal formalities take only about 15 minutes. The fee is FjD$20 and the licence is valid for 21 days.

Useful contacts
Fiji Visitors Bureau
Notcutt House
36 Southwark Bridge Road
London SE1 9EU
Tel: 020 7202 6373
Fax: 020 7928 0722
Website: www.bulafiji.com

Flight time: 21 hours
GMT: +12 hours
Visa: not required

Malaysia

Residency

You must be resident in Penang for a minimum of seven days, including the day of your arrival. If you apply for a special licence to marry, the residency requirement is waived.

Legal requirements

Proof of ID: You must produce your birth certificates (which must show names of both parents) and your passports, plus four passport-size photographs of you taken individually.

Proof of status: You will require a letter from your parish priest or a sworn affidavit confirming that you are free to marry. This then needs to be stamped by the Foreign and Commonwealth Office's Legalization Office.

Divorced: You must produce your decree absolute.

Widowed: You must produce the death certificate of your former spouse and previous marriage certificate.

Age restriction: You must be 18 years of age or over. If you are aged under 21, you must have written consent from your father in the form of a sworn affidavit.

Name change: If you have changed your name by deed poll, you must provide legal proof, stamped and signed by a solicitor. This also applies if a divorced woman reverts to her maiden name.

Ceremonies

In theory, a registered ceremony is supposed to take place in the registration office but, in practice, many registrars will allow your ceremony to be conducted in locations such as on the beach or in the grounds of your hotel. If this is not allowed, you could complete formalities in the register office and follow up with a traditional ceremony at your hotel.

Obtaining a marriage licence

The procedure for marrying in Penang involves submitting an application at the District Registration Department after the residency period. The Registrar will display a notice of your intended marriage for 21 days, after which you will be issued with a licence to marry. You marriage must take place within six months of the certificate being issued. However, it is possible to obtain a special licence that dispenses with the residency requirements. To obtain a special marriage licence, on your arrival in Penang you should submit an application to the Chief Minister's Office and request dispensation of the Notice Requirement. If the Chief Minister is satisfied with the statutory declaration and the Declaration of No Lawful Impediment, he will grant a licence for marriage, which must take place within one month.

Useful contacts
Tourism Malaysia
57 Trafalgar Square
London WC2N 5DU
Tel: 020 7930 7932
Fax: 020 7930 9015
Email: info@tourism-malaysia.co.uk
Website: www.tourismmalaysia.gov.my

Flight time: 13½ hours
GMT: +8 hours
Visa: not required

Thailand

Residency
There is a minimum residency requirement of three working days to allow time for the legal formalities to be completed.

Legal requirements
Proof of ID: You will need to provide your original birth certificates and valid ten-year passports.
Proof of status: You must complete a certificate at the British embassy in Bangkok, attesting that you are single and free to marry under Thai law.
Divorced: If either of you is divorced, you will be required to produce your decree absolute with a court stamp.

Ceremonies
Once you have fulfilled the legal proceedings, you are officially married in accordance with Thai law. After your registration is finalized, you will receive two original Thai marriage certificates, and an English translation will be given to you the following working day. This does not involve any

ceremony, and is purely a completion of administration. Some hotels can arrange for the Registrar to come to the hotel to issue the marriage certificate, and you can choose to follow the legal part of the ceremony with a traditional Buddhist wedding ceremony. Although Thailand is predominantly a Buddhist country, Christian ceremonies may be arranged.

Obtaining a marriage licence

You must complete a certificate at the British Embassy in Bangkok, attesting that you are single and free to marry under Thai law. The certificate then has to be translated into Thai (tour operators can arrange this), after which you return to the Embassy with both your British and Thai declarations and sign them in the presence of the consular officer, who will then notarize the documents. The statement and translations must then be taken to the Ministry of Foreign Affairs where the signature of the British consular officer is authenticated. This normally takes 48 hours. You can then marry at any register office anywhere in Thailand.

Useful contacts
Tourism Authority of Thailand
3rd Floor, Brook House
98–99 Jermyn Street
London SW1Y 6EE
Tel: 0870 900 2007
Fax: 020 7925 2512
Email: info@tat-uk.demon.co.uk
Website: www.thaismile.co.uk

Flight time: 12–13 hours
GMT: +7 hours
Visa: not required

The Caribbean

From the Bahamas, just off the coast of Florida, to Trinidad, just off the coast of Venezuela, the Caribbean conjures up images of laid-back island paradises of sun, sea and sand.

Package holidays still dominate the tourist industry in this part of the world, and few people attempt to organize their own weddings, preferring to leave it to the giants of the all-inclusive wedding world, such as Sandals. However, it is perfectly possible and not that difficult to organize your own wedding in the Caribbean, and if you have set your heart on one of the less visited islands, such as the British Virgin Islands, the following information could prove invaluable.

Antigua

Residency
There is no set period of residency required before the ceremony can be performed. Arrangements can begin immediately after your arrival.

Legal requirements
Proof of identity: Valid ten-year passports or birth certificates and a photograph.

Proof of status: A declaration signed in Antigua and obtained from an authorized solicitor is required.

Divorced: You must produce your original decree absolute, stamped with the seal of the court, or a certified copy.

Widowed: You must produce the death certificate of your former spouse and your previous marriage certificate.

Age restriction: All applicants should be aged 18 years or over. If you are under 18 you must provide parental consent in the form of a statutory declaration, stamped and signed by a solicitor.

Name change: If your name has been changed by deed poll you must provide legal proof, stamped and signed by a solicitor. This also applies if a divorced woman has reverted back to her maiden name.

Fees: (a) Special Licence: US $150 or EC$405, to be paid on application in Antigua.

(b) Registration fee: US$40 or EC$108.

(c) Marriage Officer: Dependent on the location selected for the ceremony.

Ceremonies

Your wedding ceremony may be performed by the Registrar or the Deputy Registrar in the Registrar's Office, or by a Civil Marriage Officer at an appointed place and time, between the hours of 6am and 8pm.

Religious ceremonies

The legal formalities required for a religious ceremony are the same as for civil ceremonies, but arrangements should be made with the appropriate church official well in advance of your arrival in Antigua, and all the documents necessary for performance of this ceremony should be provided. You should contact the Antiguan High Commission and Tourist Office for details of ministers who can perform your wedding ceremony.

Useful contacts

Antiguan High Commission
   and Tourist Office
15 Thayer Street
London W1U 3JT
Tel: 020 7486 7073/5
Fax: 020 7486 1466
Email: antbar@msn.com
Website: www.antigua-barbuda.com

Flight time: 8–10 hours
GMT: -4–5 hours
Visa: not required

Bahamas

Residency

Bahamian law states that you must both be resident in the Bahamas for 24 hours before applying for a marriage licence, and, once issued, the licence is valid for 90 days. You can write to the Registrar General at: PO Box N-532, Nassau, Bahamas or fax 001 242 322 5553. You must also produce evidence of your date of arrival in the Bahamas, that is your airline ticket or immigration card.

Legal requirements

Proof of ID: Ten-year passports valid for at least six months are required.

Proof of status: If you are single, a declaration certifying this fact must be sworn before a Notary Public or Commissioner for Oaths, and must accompany the application for the marriage licence. This declaration can also be obtained from a Notary Public in Nassau.

Divorced: The original decree absolute with a court stamp or a certified copy must be produced.

Widowed: The death certificate of your former spouse must be produced.

Age restriction: If you are aged under 18 years, parental consent in the form of a statutory declaration, stamped and signed by a solicitor, is required. Forms of consent may be obtained from the Registrar General's office in the Bahamas.

Name change: If you have changed your name by deed poll, the original copy, stamped and signed by a solicitor, is required. This also applies if you have reverted to your single name following a divorce.

Fees: The fee for a marriage licence is US$40.

Ceremonies

Bahamian wedding venues come in all shapes and sizes, from the traditional historic church to a private yacht, and from a beautiful tropical garden to the sands of Harbour Island's famous pink beach. It is even possible to exchange your vows underwater, with the fish as your witnesses and the coral as your backdrop.

Obtaining your marriage licence

Marriage licences are issued at the Office of the Registrar General, located in the Rodney Bain Building on Parliament and Shirley Street in Nassau, which is open to the public Monday to Friday between the hours of 9.30am and 4.30pm, telephone: 001 242 322 3316.

Useful contacts

Bahamas Tourist Office
10 Chesterfield Street
London W1J 5JL
Tel: 020 7355 0800
Fax: 020 7491 9459
Email: info@bahamas.co.uk
Website: www.bahamas.co.uk

Barbados

Advance arrangements

Before travelling, you must first contact the minister or magistrate who will officiate at the marriage ceremony. You will then be provided with a letter to be taken to: Ministry of Home Affairs, Level 5, General Post Office Building, Cheapside, Barbados tel: 001 246 228 8950 Fax: 001 246 437 3794. This letter must be presented at the time of filling in the application in order to obtain your marriage licence.

Residency

It is now possible for the ceremony to take place on the day of your arrival, provided that your documents are in order.

Legal requirements

Proof of ID: Original or certified copies of your birth certificates or valid passports and airline tickets.

Divorced: If either of you has been divorced, you must produce an original decree absolute.

Widowed: If either of you has been widowed, a copy of the marriage certificate or death certificate is required.

Age restriction: If you are aged under 18 years, parental consent in the form of a statutory declaration, stamped and signed by a solicitor, is required.

Name change: If your name has been changed by deed poll, legal proof, stamped and signed by a solicitor, is required. This also applies if a married woman has reverted to her maiden name.

Adopted: If you are adopted, your adoption certificate must be produced.

Ceremonies

You can have a civil or religious wedding ceremony in Barbados, whether on the beach or in a flower forest.

Documents required for marriage in a Catholic church:
• A pre-marital enquiry, completed and signed by both of you, obtainable from your parish priest.
• Baptismal certificates, issued within the last six months.
• A freedom to marry statement, signed by your parish priest.
• A certificate of participation, certifying you have taken part in a programme of preparation for marriage. In the case of a mixed religion marriage, you must obtain permission to marry or a Dispensation from Disparity of Cult, issued by the bishop of the Catholic party.
• Testimonial letters from your bishop.

Your bishop should send all these documents to:
Bishop
Diocese of Bridgetown
St Patrick's Presbytery
PO Box 1223,
Jemmotts Lane
Bridgetown
Barbados
Tel: 001 246 228 7359 or 001 246 426 2325
Fax: 001 246 429 6198

British Virgin Islands

Residency
You must be resident in the Islands for a minimum of three working days before your wedding can take place.

Legal requirements
Proof of ID: Your original birth certificates and valid ten-year passports.
Divorced: If you are divorced, you must produce your decree absolute with a court stamp.
Widowed: If you are widowed, you must provide the original of your former spouse's death certificate.
Age restriction: To marry in the British Virgin Islands you must be 18 years of age or over; otherwise parental consent must be obtained.

Ceremonies
You can choose to get married on the deck of a yacht, on a deserted sun-kissed beach, in a church of your choice, under a gazebo by the sea or in a tropical garden.

Obtaining a marriage licence
As soon as you arrive in the British Virgin Islands, you can apply for a marriage licence at the Attorney General's Office. Your licence will take three days to process and, once granted, is valid for three months from the date it is signed. You must have two witnesses to witness and sign your application form for the licence. These witnesses need not

be the same two witnesses who are present at your marriage ceremony. You may request BV Islanders to be your witnesses at the Attorney General's Office and at your wedding ceremony. Having applied for your licence, you should then go to the Registrar's Office to schedule an appointment for the date and time you want to be married. If you have made an appointment before you travelled, you will need to confirm it upon arrival. You can be married at the Registrar's Office, or outside of it. If the Registrar is required to leave the island of Tortola to go to one of the adjoining islands, you will be asked to pay his or her transport costs to that island.

Religious weddings

If you wish to be married in a church, the wedding banns must be published on three consecutive Saturdays or Sundays in the church of your choice. You must make arrangements with the minister in advance. You can get married in a church by special licence, arrangements for which must also be made with the minister.

Useful contacts

The British Virgin Islands Tourist Board
110 St Martin's Lane
London WC2N 4DY
Tel: 020 7240 4259
Fax: 020 7240 4270
Email: webmaster@bviwelcome.com
Website: www.bviwelcome.com

Cayman Islands

Residency

You can get married in the Cayman Islands from the day
of your arrival. You will need to produce a Cayman Islands
international embarkation/disembarkation card.

Legal requirements

Proof of ID: You will need to produce your original birth
certificates and valid ten-year passports.

Divorced: If either of you is divorced, you must produce
your decree absolute with a court stamp.

Widowed: If you are widowed, you will need to produce
the death certificate of your former spouse and your
previous marriage certificate.

Age restriction: The minimum age for marrying in the
Cayman Islands is 16, and anyone under 18 must have
parental consent. Consent can be given by your father, or if
he is deceased, by a lawful male guardian, or if there is no
guardian, by your mother.

Fees: The cost of a special marriage licence is CI $150 plus
a CI $10 stamp duty to accompany the documents. Stamps
may be purchased from any local post office or from the
Deputy Chief Secretary's office.

Ceremonies

There are many beautiful locations where you can have your marriage ceremony, from a quiet chapel to a shimmering white sandy beach, or even on board a ship drifting over a tranquil sea. If you would like an on-board wedding, the minister will meet you at the dock to obtain the necessary documents to process the licence. He will then go to the courthouse and return with your marriage licence.

Obtaining your marriage licence

A special marriage licence must be obtained from the Chief Secretary's Office. You must arrange for the services of a Cayman Islands Marriage Officer before applying for the licence. A list of officers is available from the Chief Secretary's Office and can be obtained before your arrival (see address below). For details of registrars and ministers who can perform your ceremony, see www.caymanislands.co.uk

Useful contacts

Cayman Islands
  Tourist Office
6 Arlington Street
London SW1A 1RE
Tel: 020 7491 7771
Fax: 020 7409 7773
Email: info-uk@caymanislands.ky
Website: www.gov.ky

Marriage Licence Application
Chief Secretary's Office
3rd Floor, Government
  Administration Building
George Town
Grand Cayman
Tel: 001 345 949 7900
Fax: 001 345 949 7544

Grenada

Residency
The minimum residency requirement before you can apply for a marriage licence is three working days, excluding weekends and bank holidays. Application for a licence can then be made at the Prime Minister's Office.

Legal requirements
Proof of ID: Your original birth certificates and valid ten-year passports are required. Also, you must provide your full names, addresses, occupations and religions, plus those of your parents.

Proof of status: An affidavit, or a letter from a clergyman, lawyer or registrar on official letterhead, attesting to the fact that you have not been married before or are free to marry.

Divorced: If you are divorced, your decree absolute with a court stamp is required.

Widowed: If you are widowed, you must provide the death certificate of your former spouse.

Name change: If your name has been changed by deed poll, you must provide legal proof, stamped and signed by a solicitor. This also applies if a married woman has reverted to her maiden name.

Adopted: If you are adopted, your adoption certificate will be required.

Age restriction: If you are aged under 21 years, parental consent is required in the form of an affidavit, stamped and signed by a solicitor.

Fees: Licence and stamp fees and copies of the marriage certificate cost EC$35.

Ceremonies

In Grenada, you may be married by a magistrate or a minister: the choice is yours, as with the location. You can choose from many locations, including a chapel, beach or the grounds of your hotel.

Obtaining a marriage licence

Application for a licence should be made at the Prime Minister's Office after the necessary stamp duty and licence fees have been paid. This process takes approximately two days (slightly longer if either of you is divorced, as your documents must then be sent to the Ministry of Legal Affairs).

Useful contacts

Grenada Board of Tourism
1 Battersea Church Road
London SW11 3LY
Tel: 020 7771 7016
Fax: 020 7771 7181
Email: grenada@cibgroup.co.uk
Website: www.grenadagrenadines.com

Jamaica

Residency
If you apply in advance for a marriage licence, you can get married 24 hours after arriving in Jamaica. Arrangements can be made through your hotel or travel agent, or directly through the Ministry of National Security and Justice.

Legal requirements
Proof of ID: Your original birth certificates, including both parents' names, and valid ten-year passports. Also full names of both sets of parents if they are not on the birth certificates.
Divorced: If you are divorced, you must produce your decree absolute.
Widowed: If either of you is widowed, you will need to produce the death certificate of your former spouse.
Age restriction: If you are aged under 21, parental consent, in the form of a statutory declaration, stamped and signed by a solicitor, is required.
Name change: If your name has been changed by deed poll, you will need to provide legal proof, stamped and signed by a solicitor. This also applies if a married woman has reverted to her maiden name.
Adopted: If you are adopted, you will need to produce the adoption certificate.

Ceremonies
You can choose to have your wedding ceremony wherever you want, be it on a beach, in the gardens of your hotel or

in a church: simply clear the location with the registrar when you apply for your marriage licence.

Obtaining a marriage licence

You can obtain your marriage licence from the Ministry of National Security and Justice direct, sending copies of all relevant documents, or you can fill in the application form on www.weddingsinjamaica.com, who will make all the arrangements for you.

Useful contacts

Jamaica Tourist Board Office
1 Prince Consort Road
London SW7 2BZ
Tel: 020 7224 0505
Fax: 020 7224 0551
Email: Jtb_uk@compuserve.com
Website: www.visitjamaica.com

St Lucia

Residency
Two days after your arrival, you can make an application for a marriage licence, which takes two days to process. It's possible to be married on the fifth day after arriving in St Lucia.

Legal requirements
Proof of ID: Your original birth certificates and valid ten-year passports.

Divorced: If either of you is divorced, you must produce the decree absolute with a court stamp.

Widowed: If you are widowed, the death certificate of your former spouse is required.

Age restriction: If either of you is under the age of 18, evidence of parental consent must be produced in the form of a notarized sworn affidavit.

Name change: If your name has been changed by deed poll, you will be required to produce legal proof stamped and signed by a solicitor. This also applies if a married woman has reverted to her maiden name.

Ceremonies
Ceremonies are all civil in St Lucia.

Obtaining a marriage licence
Application to be married in St Lucia must be made to the Attorney General, who will issue a marriage licence.

Trinidad & Tobago

Residency

The minimum residency period is three days before your wedding ceremony, and it is important to note that the day of your arrival is not counted in the three-day period.

Legal requirements

Proof of ID: You must both produce your original birth certificates and passports and proof of entry documents (airline tickets and immigration cards).

Divorced: If you are divorced, you must produce your decree absolute with a court stamp.

Widowed: If you are widowed, you must produce the death certificate of your former spouse.

Age restriction: If you are aged under 18 years, you must obtain parental consent in the form of a statutory declaration, stamped and signed by a solicitor.

Name change: If you have changed your name by deed poll, you must supply legal proof, stamped and signed by a solicitor. This also applies if you are a divorced woman and have reverted to your maiden name.

Ceremonies

Civil and church ceremonies are both possible.

Obtaining a marriage licence

You should apply for your marriage licence at the Registrar General's Office in Trinidad or the Warden's Office in Tobago.

Confetti.co.uk is the UK's leading wedding and special occasion website, helping more than 400,000 brides, grooms and guests every month.

Confetti.co.uk is packed full of ideas and advice to help organize every stage of your wedding. At confetti, you can choose from hundreds of beautiful wedding dresses; investigate our list of more than 3,000 wedding and reception venues; plan your wedding; chat to other brides about their experiences and ask for advice from Aunt Betti, our agony aunt. If your guests are online, too, we will even help you set up a wedding website to share details and photos with your family and friends.

Our extensive online content on every aspect of weddings and special occasions is now complemented by our range of books covering every aspect of planning a wedding, for everyone involved. Titles include the complete *Wedding Planner; Wedding Readings & Vows; Wedding Dresses; The Bride's Wedding; The Groom's Wedding; The Father of the Bride's Wedding; Your Daughter's Wedding; The Best Man's Wedding, Men at Weddings; How to Write a Wedding Speech* and *The Wedding Book of Calm.*

Confetti also offer:
Wedding & special occasion stationery – our stunning ranges include all the pieces you will need for all occasions, including christenings, namings, anniversaries and birthday parties.
Wedding & party products – stocking everything you need from streamers to candles to cameras to cards to flowers to fireworks and, of course, confetti!

To find out more or to order your confetti gift book, party brochure or wedding stationery brochure, visit: www.confetti.co.uk call: 0870 840 6060; email: info@confetti.co.uk
visit: Confetti, 80 Tottenham Court Road, London W1T 4TE
or Confetti, The Light, The Headrow, Leeds LS1 8TL